ASKING GREAT QUESTIONS

AN ESSENTIAL COMPANION FOR EVERY LEADER

AILEEN GIBB

Published by:
Aileen Gibb

Cover Design: Lieve Maas, www.BrightLightGraphics.com

DEDICATION

For Moe and all her questions.
And for all the clients, colleagues,
and friends who trust me with the questions
waiting to be asked.

FOREWORD
QUESTIONS BRING CLARITY

Choosing the right question is the hard part. Asking it is easy.

How much time do we spend finding the right questions? What opportunities are gained by changing one word? How are we, as leaders, developing our skills to ask spot-on questions? Questions that unlock potential, remove barriers, instil ownership and find clarity.

I met Aileen over coffee, after an acquaintance suggested we meet. My question to her that day was: "How do I build a framework for leadership in my company?" She didn't answer my question right away. Instead, Aileen posed a series of her own questions. With more questions, came great excitement as we began creating and unlocking a deep curiosity for what we could do together. How could I have known the impact a question posed to this incredible woman would have?

Over the next eighteen months, Aileen led my team on a journey to define what makes a great conversation. At its heart are questions. As we learned to ask great questions I saw that conflict led to breakthroughs. I saw individuals become inspired by their own vision of possibilities. Engagement and ownership multiplied.

Aileen opened our eyes to other worlds of thought. She taught us to ask more questions and that great leadership is knowing how to have a great conversation.

This little book in your hand is the most powerful leadership toolbox you will ever own. The questions contained in these pages will silence rooms, shift perspectives and expand possibilities. The greatness you will create by adopting these questions is endless.

Aileen is a master in her craft and I am thrilled that she is able to share her work with you, so that you too can shape a new world of leadership through conversation.

Karina Birch, CEO, *Rocky Mountain Soap Company*, Canmore, Alberta, Canada. 2016

INTRODUCTION
THIS IS A BOOK OF QUESTIONS

The word "question" contains the word "quest". Quests are an invitation to adventure, to exploration, to discovery of new lands. Questsopen you up to learning and growth. Quests reveal what you're capable of and ultimately transform you.

All quests start with a question. Yet questions are one of the most under utilized tools for leaders today.

Great questions will stop you in your tracks. Will make you think more deeply about what's in front of you. Will inspire you to look at challenges in new ways. Will open you up to new possibilities and to solutions you would not otherwise have considered.

Great questions create conversations. Real conversations that slow you down in the busy rush of every day and invite you to focus more clearly. Complete conversations that go deeper than the superficial chit-chat that may consume much of your day. Conversations where you take time to explore options in order to make better, more productive and often more creative decisions.

Questions invite you to approach things differently. To be curious. To look more deeply into what you're capable of creating — alone and together with your colleagues. Questions connect people and inspire curiosity about what's possible.

Questions can lead to innovation, creativity, accountability and ownership — all the things companies say are essential to success in today's fast-paced, ever-evolving, environment.

Yet questions are seldom the first thing out of a leader's mouth. Our prevailing belief is that leadership relies on having the 'right' answers, rather than on asking genuine questions. People in formal positions of leadership often feel pressure to have the solutions, to make the decisions and to take all the responsibility.

Great questions invite anyone — yes anyone — to take on the mantle of being a leader. Questions make it easier to speak up, to add your ideas, to have your thoughts heard, to hear the thoughts of other people and to take action on things you really believe are important.

Questions equip you to disrupt the status quo. To effectively challenge the way things have always been done. To explore whether the answers that have always been relied on, truly are in service of today's goals for you, your team or your business.

Questions connect people and create opportunities to learn from people who see the world from a different perspective than the one you habitually take. Questions build relationships and take conversations to deeper, more meaningful, more useful and more inspiring places.

And the best questions take you to places you've never been before — into the 'don't know' space, where you discover new possibilities that were previously hidden to you in your business and in your life. Once there, you'll find even more questions that you haven't asked before.

This is a book of questions. It's a primer to inspire you to step into conversations you might otherwise avoid. Conversations which you've always wished you could have. Conversations which you didn't know how to start.

Arranged under alphabetical topics, you can flick through this book and quickly find a question that relates to whatever situation you find yourself in.

You'll be familiar with some of the topics as things you come across every day. Other topics might seem strange, unusual or even provocative to you. Those may quite possibly be the places where you most need to be asking more questions. If the questions were easy, you'd already be using them.

Think of questions as a daily practice that invites you to be curious, creative, interested, intrigued and constantly evolving as a leader.

Find a question you haven't asked before. Ask it. Then listen carefully — very carefully — into what happens in the space your question creates. Listen in for what you haven't heard before. Slow down and wait for the unexpected to emerge. Watch for something you hadn't previously seen or heard. Prepare to be surprised.

Each topic in this book starts with a quote or a provocative statement that, in itself, invites you to consider something in a different way. You can then explore and experiment with the three categories of questions under that topic:

- questions you can use to lead a group conversation with your team, your colleagues or your family;

- questions which you can pose to another person to inspire their best possibilities at work or in their life;

- questions which invite you to take time for self-coaching, personal reflection and insight

The questions in this book will inspire you to set out on new quests with and for your team. It will open up new adventures and take your business to destinations you didn't believe were reachable. Even if you don't formally think of yourself as a leader, asking the questions in this book will bring out the leader in you.

Great Questions, combined with great listening, inspire great conversations which in turn shift relationships, transforming and creating leaders at all levels in organizations and communities. Leaders, not by virtue of position or job title. Leaders who, by asking more questions, uncover and reveal new paths along which you may travel in your quest for a better world.

It starts with you and the questions you find the courage to ask.

It starts as you turn to the next pages of this book.

TABLE OF CONTENTS
QUESTION TOPICS FOR LEADERS

THE QUESTIONS

"Face to face conversation is the most human, and humanizing, thing we do."

— Sherry Turkle, Reclaiming Conversation

ACCEPTANCE

When I accept that your thoughts, ideas,
perspectives and behaviours differ from mine,
I see us as two humans being human. Acceptance
of each other is a starting point for a genuine
relationship.

LEADING A GROUP CONVERSATION

What does it mean to be fully human in our current environment?

How might acceptance be a tool for progress?

What do we need to accept more fully?

INSPIRING A ONE-TO-ONE CONVERSATION

What do you need me to accept is right or wrong here?

Who do you need to accept this?

Where are you having trouble accepting that this is the only solution?

When do you reach the limits of what's acceptable?

How might you accept this more easily?

What if you were just to accept this?

What if you don't accept anyone else's ideas on this matter?

- -

SELF-COACHING AND REFLECTION

What can I accept about myself in this situation?

How might I accept this more easily?

Where am I having trouble accepting this is OK?

When do I reach my limits on what is acceptable?

Whose perspective am I open or not open to hearing?

What if I do accept that this is the best way forward?

What if I don't accept there's nothing more to do here?

AGREEMENT

Agreement is not consensus. Consensus is not effective agreement. Consensus often means one mind is overpowered by the many. Agreement is two connecting minds complementing each other on a trusted way forward.

LEADING A GROUP CONVERSATION

Where is consensus holding us back?

What if we don't need to reach consensus in order to take action?

What agreements are needed to move us forward?

INSPIRING A ONE-TO-ONE CONVERSATION

How might we best work together?

What needs to be clearer in our agreements?

Where do you trust me or not trust me to deliver on our agreement?

Who do you need to create a clearer agreement with?

When did you have an agreement go wrong between you and someone else?

What if you do create a stronger, clearer agreement with your team
on this project?

What if, in order to be more successful, you need to make a clearer agreement
with yourself?

- -

SELF-COACHING AND REFLECTION

When am I not clear enough in the agreements I make with other people?

What agreements might I make that would ensure I'm not disappointed or
frustrated by something?

Where might my team need a clearer agreement from me?

Who do I need to ask for an agreement on something?

How do I react when someone disagrees with me?

What if I respond with more curiosity when someone disagrees with me?

What if I don't get the agreements I need to support my daily success?

ASSERTIVENESS

"Don't wait for an extraordinary moment. Be assertive and confident to seize the moment at its very first instance. Waiting for the right moment may spoil an opportunity".

— Dr. Anil Kr Sinha

LEADING A GROUP CONVERSATION

What might be extraordinary if we seize it?

Do we prefer people to stand up and speak out or sit still and keep quiet?

What are we waiting for?

INSPIRING A ONE-TO-ONE CONVERSATION

What holds you back from being more assertive?

Who do you feel most assertive with?

Where and when are you not as assertive as you'd like to be?

When do you need to show up more assertively?

What do you like or not like about the word assertive?

What if I could help you bring out a more assertive version of yourself?

What results will you get if you don't assert yourself on this project?

- -

SELF-COACHING AND REFLECTION

What do I like about being described as assertive or non-assertive?

How would I like to be seen differently?

When or with whom is it easier for me to be assertive?

Where do I find it more difficult to be assertive?

Who would I be if I had all the assertiveness, confidence and courage I needed?

What if I didn't hold back from being assertive, confident or bold?

What if I never let myself be as assertive as I'd like to be?

AUTHENTICITY

Showing up authentically in words and actions requires both trust and risk. Authentic means being true to what you experience in each moment.

LEADING A GROUP CONVERSATION

How might our words and actions align more authentically?

What risks might we take in order to be more authentic?

Where would increased trust take us as a team?

INSPIRING A ONE-TO-ONE CONVERSATION

What does being authentic mean to you?

Where on this project might you speak up more authentically?

When might you be holding back from being fully authentic in our conversations?

How might I help you be more authentic?

Who holds you back from speaking up authentically?

What if you allowed yourself to be more authentic?

What if we could be more authentic as a team and as a business?

- -

SELF-COACHING AND REFLECTION

How do I behave when I'm truly authentic?

What results do I get when I'm being authentic?

How authentic am I being?

What might be holding me back from being more authentic?

Who is the most authentic person I know? What makes them so?

What if I could show up more authentically — how would I be different?

What if other people don't see me as authentic?

AUTHORITY

Be author-like rather than authoritative. Author your conversations from spirit rather than from positional power.

LEADING A GROUP CONVERSATION

When are our conversations authored from spirit?

Where are our conversations authored by positional power?

Which will serve us better going forward?

INSPIRING A ONE-TO-ONE CONVERSATION

What will you do to claim all the authority you need in this situation?

Whose authority do you need to move this project/situation forward?

When do you need more authority?

Where might you approach authority differently in order to be even more successful?

How do you stop yourself from claiming your authority?

What if you already have all the authority you need?

What if it's not about being in authority at all?

- -

SELF-COACHING AND REFLECTION

Who would I be in the eyes of other people if I couldn't rely on, or hide behind my job title?

What permission do I give myself to author my own story?

How do I connect with other stories in my team or business?

When do I most effectively use my natural authority?

Where might I not be using my power to full impact?

What if I more willingly gave up my perceived authority?

What if people perceive me to have greater or less authority than I think I have?

AWARENESS

Those who know not and know not that they know not are asleep, let them slumber.

Those who know not and know that they know not, are awakening, guide them.

Those who know and know not that they know, are awake, be a light unto their dawning.

Those who know and know that they know, are wise ones, learn from them.

— Adaptation of a Persian Proverb

LEADING A GROUP CONVERSATION

Where are our blindspots?

What don't we know right now?

How will we find out what we don't yet know?

What questions would enhance our awareness?

INSPIRING A ONE-TO-ONE CONVERSATION

What are you aware of that caused this situation to arise?

How aware are you of how your words and actions affect other people?

Where might you not be aware of something important?

When did you shift your awareness on this?

Who else needs to be aware of what you know?

What if there's more to be aware of here?

What if you aren't aware of the full situation?

- -

SELF-COACHING AND REFLECTION

How aware am I of what other people are thinking or feeling about things?

Where do I need to be more aware of how my words and actions impact other people?

When might I be less aware of what's happening than I need to be?

Who might have more awareness of this situation than I do?

What might I not be aware of in this situation? What questions do I need to ask?

What if I am missing something here?

What if there's something no one is aware of that's important?

BALANCE

Balance invites us to slow down and integrate all the jewels in our kaleidoscope of life.

LEADING A GROUP CONVERSATION

What does balance really mean for us?

What are the jewels in our kaleidoscope of life?

What will a more integrated life look like?

INSPIRING A ONE-TO-ONE CONVERSATION

How are you feeling at this time about the balance between your work and home priorities?

What feels off balance for you just now?

Where might you balance the amount of time you spend talking versus listening?

When do you need to balance all the ideas of your team members?

Who do you need to ask for help to balance things better?

What if you truly live a more balanced life?

What if there is no way to find real balance?

- -

SELF-COACHING AND REFLECTION

How balanced was my listening versus my talking today?

Where did I balance the input from all my team members today?

When are my ideas out of balance with those of other people?

Where was the balance of my thinking today?

Who do I need to ask for help to balance things better?

What if I better balance my home and work priorities?

What if I make a different choice to better balance my priorities tomorrow?

BEHAVIOURS

People respond to how you act and behave more than they respond to what you say.

LEADING A GROUP CONVERSATION

What do our behaviours convey to other people?

How might we behave differently for greater results?

Where might we better align our words and actions?

INSPIRING A ONE-TO-ONE CONVERSATION

What do I do that impacts you positively or negatively?

What behaviours are key to your success on this project?

Where do you need to keep learning in order to get better results?

How are you getting feedback on your behaviour as a team player?

Whose behaviour is troubling you at this time?

What if you don't change your behaviour?

What if your behaviour is the result of stress or pressure?

- -

SELF-COACHING AND REFLECTION

Where are my behaviours not aligned with what I say?

What behaviour serves me best as a leader?

When might I ask for feedback on how people experience my behaviour as a leader?

What do I need when stress or pressure results in ineffective behaviour on my part?

How might I develop even better leadership behaviours?

What if my behaviour is getting in the way of success?

What if I don't change a behaviour that's not serving me well?

BEING A LEADER VERSUS DOING MANAGEMENT

Managing pre-supposes a need for control over people and results. Leading means inspiring people to create results for themselves. Managing and leading are different mindsets

LEADING A GROUP CONVERSATION

Which mindset – managing or leading – will serve to create sustainable success?

How might we create more leaders?

What results do we seek to inspire?

INSPIRING A ONE-TO-ONE CONVERSATION

Where do you get bogged down in managing details?

How might you step up and lead more?

When do you want to take more of a leadership role?

Who might take a lead on this?

What do you need to take on more of a leadership role?

What if you didn't have to manage on this project?

What if you work more in harmony with your leadership strengths?

- -

SELF-COACHING AND REFLECTION

How much of my time is spent leading versus doing tasks?

What do I need to do to change this balance?

Where might I manage less and lead more?

When do I get in my own way?

To whom might I delegate more of my tasks?

What if I didn't have to manage the details on this project?

What if I could spend more time leading strategically?

BOLDNESS

Don't be old, be bold. Old ideas, thoughts, patterns, assumptions hold you back from pushing yourself to your edge, taking a risk, or discovering you are more than you thought. Boldness finds the surprise waiting over the horizon.

LEADING A GROUP CONVERSATION

What old patterns might we need to give up?

Where might we be bolder in our thoughts and actions?

How might we discover what's beyond our known horizon?

INSPIRING A ONE-TO-ONE CONVERSATION

How might I help you take bolder steps?

What's holding you back from being as bold as you'd like to be?

When you do step up boldly how does it feel?

Where would you like to be bolder?

Who do you admire for their boldness? What might you learn from them?

What if you allowed yourself to say the boldest thing you'd like to say to me?

What if you are the only one limiting your boldness?

- -

SELF-COACHING AND REFLECTION

Where might I have been bolder today?

What's happening tomorrow that might call me to boldness?

How do I feel when I take a bold step?

When do I hold back from being as bold as I'd like to be?

With whom might I speak up more boldly?

What if I take the boldest step I can think of on this project?

What if I don't let anything hold me back — where might I boldly 'go'?

CHALLENGE

To remain indifferent to the challenges we face is indefensible. If the goal is noble, whether or not it is realized within our lifetime is largely irrelevant. What we must do therefore is to strive and persevere and never give up.

— Dalai Lama XIV

LEADING A GROUP CONVERSATION

What new challenge might we take on?

How might we create a more noble goal?

What inspires us to never give up?

INSPIRING A ONE-TO-ONE CONVERSATION

What are you finding challenging on this project?

Where do you have a specific challenge with this?

Who do you need to help you with this challenge?

How might you overcome this challenge?

When have you faced and overcome a similar challenge?

What if you are making this more challenging than it needs to be?

What if this could be a really exciting challenge?

- -

SELF-COACHING AND REFLECTION

What is it I'm challenged by in this situation?

Why do I feel challenged by this?

How might I face up to this challenge?

When have I overcome a similar challenge in the past and what did I learn that might help me here?

Where am I most excited by the challenges ahead?

Who can help me with this challenge?

What if I'm making this more challenging than it really is?

What if I can't overcome this challenge?

CHOICE

"Between stimulus and response there is a space. In that space is our power to choose our response. In our response lies our growth and our freedom."

— Viktor E. Frankl

LEADING A GROUP CONVERSATION

If we created more space, what different choices might we make?

What choice will lead us to growth and freedom?

What would be the most unexpected choice we might make?

INSPIRING A ONE-TO-ONE CONVERSATION

How might you make a different choice with better results?

Where are you struggling to make a choice?

When did you make a choice that worked out better than you thought it would?

Who will be affected by this choice?

What other choices might be open to you here?

What if you made a different choice right now?

What if there is no other choice to be made on this?

- -

SELF-COACHING AND REFLECTION

Where might I not be making the best choice for myself?

What if I made a different choice here?

Whose approval do I need in order to choose a different approach to this?

How might I make better choices for myself?

When have I made a choice I regretted?

What if there's another choice open to me on this?

What if this is the only choice I need to make?

COMMITMENT

"Real commitment is heartfelt allegiance to that gift which brings you and others alive."

— David Whyte

**"anything or anyone
that does not bring you alive
is too small for you."**

— David Whyte, Poem: Sweet Darkness

LEADING A GROUP CONVERSATION

To what do we give our heartfelt commitment?

By making this commitment, what else are we saying no to?

What brings us truly alive?

What calls us to play bigger?

INSPIRING A ONE-TO-ONE CONVERSATION

Where are you putting most of your commitment these days?

What are you really committed to achieving here?

When do you feel you are less committed than you might be?

Where does your commitment increase and why?

How might you increase your commitment to this project?

What if this is not what you need to commit yourself to?

What if you fully committed to only this project?

- -

SELF-COACHING AND REFLECTION

What am I truly committed to?

Whose commitment do I need on this project?

How might I commit more to this goal?

Where do I notice my commitment waning?

When do I not bring my full commitment into play?

What if I'm not committed to this any more?

What if I could garner more commitment for this?

COMPASS

Compass, most commonly used as a noun, can also take the form of a verb. To compass something means to extend, encircle, stretch, attain, accomplish or achieve.

LEADING A GROUP CONVERSATION

Where is our current direction taking us?

How do we need to reorientate?

What would compass and stretch us in a positive way?

How might we expand our circle of influence?

INSPIRING A ONE-TO-ONE CONVERSATION

What direction are you headed in with this project?

When will you know you're successful with this?

Where is this taking you?

Who do you need to bring along with you on this matter?

How will you know when you've succeeded with this?

What if there's another way to go with this?

What if you could steer this to success more quickly?

- -

SELF-COACHING AND REFLECTION

What serves as my leadership compass?

Which principles do I rely on to keep me on course?

When do I get pulled off course?

Where is this direction taking me and my team?

Where am I heading?

What if there's another way to go with this?

What if this isn't going to lead to success?

COMPASSION

"Compassion is not a relationship between the healer and the wounded. It's a relationship between equals. Compassion becomes real when we recognize our shared humanity."

— Pema Chödrön, The Places that Scare You

LEADING A GROUP CONVERSATION

How might we act more as equals?

Where might we recognize more of our shared humanity?

Where or with whom might we practice greater compassion?

INSPIRING A ONE-TO-ONE CONVERSATION

Who might you show more compassion for?

When do you experience the most compassion?

Where are we not being compassionate enough in our company?

How do you show compassion?

What does compassion mean to you?

What if you were more compassionate on this?

What if compassion is not what's needed here?

- -

SELF-COACHING AND REFLECTION

Where might I have shown more compassion today?

How might I bring more compassion into my world?

When do people need my compassion most?

Who last showed me some compassion?

What does being compassionate really look like to me?

What if I brought more compassion to this situation?

What if I don't experience more compassion for this person?

COMMUNICATION

When people say: "We need better communication around here" or "They need to communicate better", ask who "they" are. Don't complain, step up and explain. Start the conversation. It's in you to communicate!

LEADING A GROUP CONVERSATION

How might we step up and ask for the communication we need?

What if we didn't hold back, waiting for someone else to communicate?

What do we want to communicate more openly and to whom?

INSPIRING A ONE-TO-ONE CONVERSATION

What suggestions do you have for me to improve my communication style?

How might you communicate better with other people?

Where do you need to share an important communication with other people?

What's missing from our regular communications?

When do you get scared or worried about communicating?

What if you are a really strong communicator?

What if you don't address the difficulties you have communicating
with other people?

- -

SELF-COACHING AND REFLECTION

Where was I most effective or ineffective in my communication today?

What important message do I need to communicate and to whom?

With whom am I avoiding an important communication?

When might I be a better communicator?

How well did I listen to communications from other people today?

What if I missed something in today's communications?

What if communicating, whatever the message, were always enjoyable?

CONFLICT

The problem with conflict is that we LABEL it conflict. Shift to curiosity and ask what's really going on inside. Be curious to understand the other person and the conflict melts away.

LEADING A GROUP CONVERSATION

What will it take to shift from conflict to curiosity?

How might doing so make us a stronger team?

What conflicts might curiosity free us from?

INSPIRING A ONE-TO-ONE CONVERSATION

How might you look at this conflict situation in a different way?

What do you need to move through or beyond this conflict?

Where might you have inadvertently created or contributed to this conflict?

When has a conflict made you feel emotional?

With whom are you willing to resolve a conflict?

What if you can lead yourself and your team to approach this conflict situation in a better way?

What if you don't learn something from this conflict situation?

- -

SELF-COACHING AND REFLECTION

Where did I avoid or hide from a potential conflict today?

How might I better handle a conflict conversation?

What will it take for me to move from conflict to curiosity?

When do I see something good coming from conflict?

With whom am I ready to risk creating conflict?

What if I inadvertently caused a conflict situation today?

What if I didn't label this situation as a conflict?

CONNECTING

- -

Start every conversation listening for that which connects you with each other. We are more alike than we like to think.

- -

LEADING A GROUP CONVERSATION

What really connects us as a team?

Where might we reach out and connect more with other people?

What important connections are we missing?

INSPIRING A ONE-TO-ONE CONVERSATION

Where might you be missing an important connection on this project?

Who might you connect with to get more done on this?

When do you hold back from connecting with other people and why is that?

How might you increase your circle of connections on this?

What do you need to connect other people into this project?

What if there is no meaningful connection with you on this?

What if you were to connect those ideas?

- -

SELF-COACHING AND REFLECTION

What connection might I be missing here?

Who do I need to connect with more often?

Where do I avoid making a connection with someone?

When do I feel most connected or disconnected to what's important?

How might I explore different ways to connect with other people?

What if there's someone important I could connect with on this?

What if I don't make any connections with new people?

CONVERSATION

- -

Ninety-nine percent of conversations in our busy lives are incomplete.

- -

LEADING A GROUP CONVERSATION

What will it take to slow down and complete our conversations?

What will we gain by doing so?

How will we make face to face conversation a priority?

INSPIRING A ONE-TO-ONE CONVERSATION

What's been the best conversation you've had recently?

Where might you create more powerful conversations and with whom?

Who are you avoiding a conversation with?

When will you step into that conversation with your colleagues?

How might you improve your conversation skills?

What if you were brave enough to have the most honest conversation you could with that person?

What if you don't say anything?

- -

SELF-COACHING AND REFLECTION

Who do I need a full conversation with?

What opportunities for full conversation am I creating or avoiding?

Where would a more complete conversation have served better today?

When might I next create a powerful conversation and for what reason?

How might I improve my conversation skills?

What if I brought everyone into one big conversation about this issue?

What if I continued down this path without any further conversation?

DECISION MAKING

We make decisions into huge multi-armed monsters, when in reality, as human beings we make millions of tiny, cumulative decisions every second. In that sense decision-making is the essence of living

(heard on podcast?)

LEADING A GROUP CONVERSATION

What decision are we making into monsters?

What decisions feel most human to us?

What decisions do we need to challenge in order to reach our goal?

INSPIRING A ONE-TO-ONE CONVERSATION

What do you need in order to make this decision?

How would you proceed here if the decision were up to you?

Who else might need to be involved in or consulted with on this decision?

Where are you ready to take on more decisions?

What if you made this decision?

What if you are hesitating to make a decision on this?

SELF-COACHING AND REFLECTION

Who is best placed to make this decision?

What decision do I currently hesitate to make?

How do I hang on to decisions which other people could make?

When have I made a decision that didn't work out as I expected?

What if I make a risky decision and it turned out OK?

What if I hold off making a decision?

EMPATHY

"The empathic relationship does not begin with "I know how you feel" — it begins with the realization you don't know how another person feels."

— Rowan Williams, former Archbishop of Canterbury

"Empathy needs face-to-face conversation and eye contact."

— Sherry Turkle, Reclaiming Conversation

LEADING A GROUP CONVERSATION

What if we were to ask how our colleagues and customers really feel?

What questions invite us to be more empathic with each other?

Who do we need to meet with in person in order to see eye to eye with them?

INSPIRING A ONE-TO-ONE CONVERSATION

Who is the most empathic person you work with?

What would it take for you to show more empathy to others?

How do you feel when someone shows empathy towards you?

When might I need to be show more empathy to you and your team?

Where would empathy be a better approach for you to take?

What if you were known for showing empathy?

- -

SELF-COACHING AND REFLECTION

Who might need me to show more empathy?

What might showing more empathy say about me as a leader?

How might I be more empathic towards other people?

When do I feel challenged to show empathy?

Where would showing more empathy serve people better?

What if I were to be known as an empathic leader?

E

ENGAGEMENT

Organizations don't engage people. People engage themselves. Choose to engage in a meaningful way. Engage yourself.

LEADING A GROUP CONVERSATION

Where do we create more meaningful engagement?

What does being all in mean for us?

How might we invite our colleagues or clients to engage more fully with our work?

INSPIRING A ONE-TO-ONE CONVERSATION

How engaged are you in this project — are you all in?

Where might you engage more with others in order to achieve success?

Who are you not engaging with and why?

When do you feel most engaged in this project or business?

What do you need to engage more fully in this situation?

If you were *all in* and fully engaged, what would be different?

If you didn't engage in this situation, what else would you do?

- -

SELF-COACHING AND REFLECTION

Where did I feel most engaged in work today?

Who might I need to engage further in this project or task?

How might I have better engaged people in this situation?

What drives me to engage fully in this challenge?

When might I be holding back from fully engaging with other people?

What if everyone were fully engaged on this goal?

What if no one wants to engage in this project?

EXCELLENCE

Reaching beyond what's average or mediocre, we encounter the value of striving for excellence.

LEADING A GROUP CONVERSATION

Where might we move beyond average or mediocre?

How willing are we to strive for real excellence?

Why are we settling for less than we know ourselves to be worthy of?

INSPIRING A ONE-TO-ONE CONVERSATION

What does excellence look like for you?

Where do you feel you've done your most excellent work so far?

What do you need to bring out the excellence in yourself and in your team?

What's getting in the way of true excellence on this?

When do you allow yourself to be ok with less than excellent?

What if you could truly excel at this?

What if you don't need to be excellent all the time?

- -

SELF-COACHING AND REFLECTION

Where did I see excellence today?

How did I reach for excellence today?

What does excellence really look like on this project?

When do I see excellence emerging in my team?

Where might I not have taken that extra step towards excellence today?

What if I give myself permission for things not to be excellent?

What if, in looking for excellence, I might be missing something else?

EXPECTATIONS

Hold only one expectation: to bring all your initiative, creativity, ideas, skills, talent and courage to make this the best work you'll ever do — and do everything you can to help our clients do the same.

- IC International Role Description

LEADING A GROUP CONVERSATION

How are we bringing all our initiative, creativity, ideas, skills, talent and courage together?

What if we expect the unexpected?

How well are we responding to other people's expectations of our team?

INSPIRING A ONE-TO-ONE CONVERSATION

What do you understand is expected of you in this task or project?

Where do you feel expectations are unreasonable?

How might you be clearer in your expectations of other people?

When do expectations inspire and excite you?

Whose expectations need to be clearer for you?

What if you are expecting too much?

What if you are placing too many expectations on yourself?

- -

SELF-COACHING AND REFLECTION

Where might I be expecting too much of other people?

When might I expect too much of myself?

Who has disappointed me in not meeting my expectations?

How might I approach or look at expectations differently?

What expectations do my team have of me as a leader?

What if my expectations are unreasonable?

What if I let go of my expectations of how people do their work?

FAILURE

Put the 'I' into failure by asking "What's my hand in this." Put the 'L' into failure by learning to make it better.

LEADING A GROUP CONVERSATION

How far are we prepared to go before failing?

What are we truly learning from our failures?

How might failure make us more creative?

INSPIRING A ONE-TO-ONE CONVERSATION

Who do you know who has failed at this same task and what might you learn from them?

Where are you most concerned that you might fail?

When did you last experience failure and what happened?

How do you feel at the prospect of failing on this?

What is your biggest failure in life or work so far and how did you move on from it?

If you let this project or task fail, what might happen?

If you can't control this situation and it fails, what might you learn?

SELF-COACHING AND REFLECTION

How do I react to the thought of failing?

When did I last really fail at something and what did I learn?

Where am I facing the possibility of failure at this time?

What am I really scared of failing at?

Who do I ask for help when I personally fail at something?

What if I let this project or task fail, what might happen?

What if I don't ever let myself fail, who will I become?

FEAR

- -

Fear may be the edge that leads you through challenge to innovation. Fearing less makes you fearless.

- -

LEADING A GROUP CONVERSATION

What feels like the scariest way forward for us?

What edge is this fear leading us to?

If we are not afraid of fear what next step will we take?

What might lie on the other side of this fear?

INSPIRING A ONE-TO-ONE CONVERSATION

What's your biggest fear about this task or project?

How might I help you overcome your current fear?

When have you faced a fear and overcome it successfully?

Where is fear holding you back?

What exactly are you afraid of in this situation?

What if you had no fear about this, what would your next step be?

What if you are ignoring an important fear?

- -

SELF-COACHING AND REFLECTION

What am I most afraid of at this time?

When do I let fear hold me back?

Where am I ignoring or avoiding some fear?

Who would I become if I did not let my fears derail me?

How might I best overcome and address my current fears?

What If I had no fear about this task or project, what would be my next step?

What if my fear is real?

FEEDBACK

- -

As a leader seek feedback more often than you give it. People around you will adopt your enthusiasm for learning and growth

- -

LEADING A GROUP CONVERSATION

What feedback are we resistant to hearing?

What's working, going well, exciting us?

Where might we upgrade, change or improve to get better results?

How might we use this feedback to move forward?

INSPIRING A ONE-TO-ONE CONVERSATION

How open are you to receiving feedback on this?

Where would you like feedback from me?

When did you share positive feedback with your team?

What is the best feedback you could hear about?

Who would you value hearing some feedback from?

What if there's important feedback you need to hear about?

What if you don't ask for feedback from your team on this?

- -

SELF-COACHING AND REFLECTION

Where do I need to ask for feedback at this time?

What's holding me back from asking for feedback on this?

How does it feel when I receive negative feedback?

Who do I need to give some positive feedback at this time?

When have I not delivered feedback very well and how might I do it differently?

What if someone is holding back from giving me feedback on this?

What if I don't want to hear what the real feedback is for me here?

FOCUS

Focus is the new superpower. Overworked, under-resourced organizations end up doing many things half-well, rather than focusing on a few things to do really well.

LEADING A GROUP CONVERSATION

What is the one thing we will focus on to really make the difference?

Which few things do we need to do really well?

With focus as our super-power what will we create?

INSPIRING A ONE-TO-ONE CONVERSATION

What needs your focus at this time?

Who is distracting you from focusing on what's most important?

How might I help you focus more clearly?

Where are you putting your main focus on this project?

When might you shift focus to get different results?

What if we focus our efforts better as a team?

What if you lose focus on what's important?

- -

SELF-COACHING AND REFLECTION

Where did I put my focus today and what did I create as a result?

Who or what pulled me off focus today and how might I avoid that in future?

What one thing, if I focus on it, will make a big difference?

How well am I focussing my team's attention on what's important?

Where do I need to focus more?

What if I focus on one important thing just now?

What if I shift my focus to create better results?

F

GRIEVANCES

Blame, complain or reframe. You are both the source of, and the solution to, your own grievances.

LEADING A GROUP CONVERSATION

How might we be creating grief for ourselves?

If we stop complaining, what else might we try?

Where do we need to accept responsibility and move on?

INSPIRING A ONE-TO-ONE CONVERSATION

When are you experiencing some degree of grief?

Where is your grievance really coming from regarding this project, task or team?

How might you take steps to find a solution to this grievance?

What's at the real root of this grievance for you?

Who else is experiencing this type of grievance?

What if you could resolve this grievance?

What if you are causing the grievance?

- -

SELF-COACHING AND REFLECTION

What's causing me grief at this time?

How might I let go of what is causing me grief?

Where might I better respond to a grievance?

When did I do or say something to cause grief in other people today?

Whose grievances am I open or not open to hearing?

What if I'm trying to solve other people's grievances, rather than empowering and equipping them to resolve it themselves?

What if I am causing the grief in this situation?

GROWING PEOPLE AND PERFORMANCE

Leaders grow the business. The business grows leaders. Businesses grow at the rate leaders grow. If your business or project is stalled, go grow yourself.

LEADING A GROUP CONVERSATION

What fuels our growth as a team?

Why do we need to grow any more?

Where do we see ultimate growth taking us?

INSPIRING A ONE-TO-ONE CONVERSATION

Where do you want to grow your skills, talents and contribution?

What is holding back your growth at this time?

How might I support you better in your growth?

When do feel you have grown most in the past month or year?

What opportunity do you see for personal growth on this task or project?

What if you want to contribute more to the company's and team's growth?

What if your pace of growth is too slow?

- -

SELF-COACHING AND REFLECTION

How did I grow today?

When did I see growth in other people today?

What opportunities for growth did I miss or avoid today?

Where will my next steps on growth come from?

How might I have outgrown this role or relationship?

What if I achieve my personal growth goals?

What if something is stunting or holding back my growth at this time?

HAPPINESS

"It is by being fully involved with every detail of our lives, whether good or bad, that we find happiness."

— Mihaly Csikszentmihalyi, *FLOW*

LEADING A GROUP CONVERSATION

How does our work bring us joy and happiness?

How might we create more happiness for our colleagues and clients?

How might we find the silver lining in the smallest of everyday things?

INSPIRING A ONE-TO-ONE CONVERSATION

When are you happiest at work?

How happy are you about this decision?

Where do you get pulled away from what makes you happy?

What might you do to create more happiness for your team or your colleagues or yourself?

How happy is your team at this time?

What if I could support you in creating increased happiness?

What if you got clearer on what happiness really means to you?

- -

SELF-COACHING AND REFLECTION

When do I experience true happiness?

What pulls me away from being happy?

How might I increase happiness in my life or work?

Whose happiness did I impact today?

Where could I create more happiness in my team and in my business?

What if I could be even happier?

What if I'm not as happy as I'd like to be with this situation?

HEALTH

Healthy people make healthy leaders. Healthy leaders inspire healthy teams. Healthy teams create a healthy business. A healthy business starts with healthy conversations.

LEADING A GROUP CONVERSATION

What would be a healthy conversation for us to have as a team?

What would increase our health as a team?

How might we take a more healthy perspective on success?

INSPIRING A ONE-TO-ONE CONVERSATION

What is affecting your health at this time?

How healthy is your team now?

What would create a healthier environment on this task or project?

Where might you be missing part of the whole perspective on this?

When do you need to step back, relax, review or take a fresh look at things?

What if we had a healthy conversation about this task or project?

What if this is not a healthy approach to things?

- -

SELF-COACHING AND REFLECTION

How healthy do I feel after today's challenges and achievements?

What might I do to be healthier tomorrow?

When do I feel unhealthy, even toxic?

Where or with whom was I less than healthy today?

What pulled me off my health commitments today?

What if I made more time to relax, renew and re-energize?

What if things weren't so unhealthy around here?

H

HEARING

- -

Relationships are built not on what's said, but on what's heard, received, and acted upon.

- -

LEADING A GROUP CONVERSATION

What are we really hearing from our sponsors, clients and colleagues?

How are we receiving what we don't want to hear?

What have we heard that we need to act upon more quickly?

INSPIRING A ONE-TO-ONE CONVERSATION

What did you hear in what I just said?

Where are you hearing something differently from me?

When you really listen to yourself, what do you hear?

How is your hearing influenced by your past experience on this?

When would you like to be heard more clearly?

What if I'm not hearing you properly?

What if you could get everyone to hear what you're saying about this?

- -

SELF-COACHING AND REFLECTION

When might I not have heard correctly today?

Where might I have heard something I didn't like?

Who do I have trouble really hearing?

What am I hearing beyond the obvious words in this situation?

How is my hearing influenced by my own judgement, assumptions or bias?

What if I'm not being heard the way I think I am?

What if I were to hear more suggestions from others?

H

I-VOICE

Taking the 'I' out of TEAM means losing the uniqueness of each person. Listen for each 'I' voice to speak and connect eye to eye (or I to I).

LEADING A GROUP CONVERSATION

How well do we honour each person's contribution to our team?

Whose talent might we unleash for greater value?

How might we better combine our individual talents to create something greater together?

Whose voice is yet to be heard more strongly?

INSPIRING A ONE-TO-ONE CONVERSATION

What is your individual perspective or opinion on this?

What do you need me to hear about this situation?

How might I create more opportunities for you to speak up in your own voice?

Where might it serve you better to express more of your opinion or ideas?

What are you not yet expressing that might be useful for me to hear?

What if you hold back from expressing your true thoughts or perspective?

What if you don't say "I" more often?

- -

SELF-COACHING AND REFLECTION

Where, when or with whom do I need to express my perspective, opinions or ideas more powerfully?

Where, when or with whom do I hold back from using my I-voice?

When do I hide behind the use of the generic we?

How might I speak up with my I-voice more often?

What do I need to be able to use my I-voice more?

What if I would use my I-voice more effectively?

What if I don't bring my I-voice more into the world?

INSPIRATION

Inspiration means to breathe life into. Motivation means getting someone to do something you want them to do. Inspiration means creating the environment where people create because they want to.

— Adapted from Lance Secretan, Reclaiming Higher Ground.

LEADING A GROUP CONVERSATION

What truly inspires us?

How do we turn that inspiration into results?

Where and how might we breathe new life into our work?

INSPIRING A ONE-TO-ONE CONVERSATION

When are you most inspired?

How might you describe the spirit of our team, company, community
at this time?

Where would you breath new life into this task or project?

What do you truly want to do, be and create?

What if you could fulfill your heart's desire?

What if you could experience true inspiration?

- -

SELF-COACHING AND REFLECTION

When am I most inspired?

What would breathe new life into me, my team, my business, or my community
at this time?

How do I know what people truly want to do, be and create?

What do I truly want to do, be and create in my life or work?

What if I could fulfill my heart's desire?

What if I could better inspire my team, business or my community at this time?

JAZZ

Leadership is jazz. The foundation principles of listening, paying attention, asking questions and valuing people, allow the rhythm of each conversation to play out and be heard. It's about flow and response rather than command and control. It's about dancing in the moment and being surprised and delighted by what you hear.

LEADING A GROUP CONVERSATION

What music or rhythm describes us?

What are the foundational principles that underpin our work?

How might we surprise and delight ourselves and other people?

INSPIRING A ONE-TO-ONE CONVERSATION

What might happen if you were open to giving up some control
on this project?

Where might you listen more deeply to what's being created by your team?

What question wants to be asked at this time?

Who do you admire for their flowing, creative style of leadership?

What leadership principles are key to success on this task or project?

What if you were even more creative?

What if you created space for new ideas to emerge on this topic?

- -

SELF-COACHING AND REFLECTION

Where did I seek to be in too much control today?

When and with whom might I have listened more deeply and tuned in to what
was being said?

What are the three principles that enable me to respond as a leader?

Who do I admire for their "jazz" approach to leadership?

How might I learn to create more leadership jazz in my work?

What if I were to dance more with that key question?

What if I don't go with the flow here?

J

KINDNESS

- -

"Kind is the new cool"

— seen on a t-shirt slogan

- -

LEADING A GROUP CONVERSATION

How does our work contribute to a kind world?

What if we were kinder to ourselves and to our customers?

How might kindness be a strength ?

K

INSPIRING A ONE-TO-ONE CONVERSATION

What does kindness mean to you?

Where might you show more kindness?

Who shows you most kindness and how do they do so?

When do you demonstrate kindness?

How might we be more kind as a team or organization?

What if you could experience more kindness in your work or in your life?

What if kindness were your only focus?

- -

SELF-COACHING AND REFLECTION

Where did I lead with kindness today?

What opportunities do I have to show more kindness?

Where do I find it challenging to be kinder?

When do I experience kindness in others?

What if kindness were my main driver?

What if more kindness were what's needed in my life and in my work?

K

KNOWLEDGE

Living in the "don't know" space, invites a deeper knowing to enhance our knowledge.

LEADING A GROUP CONVERSATION

What don't we know?

How might we uncover what we don't yet know?

What if we admit we don't know everything?

What deeper knowing might we learn to love?

INSPIRING A ONE-TO-ONE CONVERSATION

What might you not know here?

Where might you find out more about this?

Who do you consider to have the most knowledge about this situation?

What knowledge does your team need to be successful with this and where might they find it?

Who do you need to learn from?

What if you trust your deepest knowing here?

What if you don't know what's true in this situation?

- -

SELF-COACHING AND REFLECTION

What do I really need to know or not to know about this situation?

Where did I gain really important knowledge today?

When might I not need to know as much as I think I need?

Who knows better than I do on this situation?

What knowledge might I truly need to pass on to others to ensure their success?

What if I'm working from out-of-date knowledge?

What if I don't trust my deepest knowing in this moment?

K

LEADERSHIP

- -

Leaders often become leaders to pursue and explore a vital question that follows them for life.

- -

LEADING A GROUP CONVERSATION

What is the question we are pursuing together?

What questions have followed each of us in our lives?

How do our questions transform us into leaders?

INSPIRING A ONE-TO-ONE CONVERSATION

Where are you willing to take on more leadership?

What do you need to be able to step up more as a leader?

What does being a leader mean to you?

How do other people experience you as a leader?

Where do you hold back from taking a leadership role?

What if you were the only one ready to take a lead here, what would you do next?

What if you let other people see you more as a leader?

- -

SELF-COACHING AND REFLECTION

Where did I step up and show leadership today?

What holds me back from being a leader?

How and where might I take on more of a leadership role?

What does being a leader really mean to me?

Where did I demonstrate effective leadership today?

What if leadership is more challenging than I think?

What if I'm not ready to be a leader?

L

LEARNING

Leadership is learning through new adventures, through failure, experimenting and testing new ways.

LEADING A GROUP CONVERSATION

What have we learned from our past efforts that will help us

move forward now?

What new adventure does learning open up for us?

Where can we experiment more?

L

INSPIRING A ONE-TO-ONE CONVERSATION

What do you need to learn in order to be successful on this task or project?

When did you have your biggest learning recently?

Who do you need to learn from?

What's your biggest learning challenge and what do you need to overcome it?

How might you capture your learning from this?

What if you help your colleagues with their learning?

What if you and your team don't learn from this situation?

- -

SELF-COACHING AND REFLECTION

What did I learn about myself today?

What did I learn about other people today?

How did I share my learning with other people today?

Where might I need to learn further in order to get better results?

Where did I help myself and other people learn today?

What if I translate my learning today into a sustainable practice or process?

What if I get input from other people on what I could learn to do better?

L

LISTENING

Listening is respect in action.

— Keith Massie, first client of IC International

LEADING A GROUP CONVERSATION

What are we listening for?

What is calling to be heard?

How might we enjoy more listening space where we inspire creative
unfolding and expansion?

INSPIRING A ONE-TO-ONE CONVERSATION

How, where and with whom might you listen better?

What did you hear when you really listened well to your team?

To whom do you find it difficult to listen well?

Who do you admire as a listener in your life?

How might you practice better listening daily?

What if you need me to hear something more about this?

What if listening were easy for you?

- -

SELF-COACHING AND REFLECTION

How, where and with whom might I practice better listening?

When do I listen well and when do I fail to listen well enough?

How might I adopt a daily practice of better listening?

Who did I listen to and learn from today?

Where might I have listened better today?

What if better listening would serve me and others?

What if I'm not listening as well as I need to?

L

LOVE

To be in love with your work is an act of sublime service to your life's purpose.

LEADING A GROUP CONVERSATION

What keeps us in love with our work?

Where might we show more love to each other, our colleagues and our clients?

What greater purpose do we love to express?

L

INSPIRING A ONE-TO-ONE CONVERSATION

What do you love to do the most?

Where are the opportunities to do more of what you love?

How loving do you consider we are as a team, as a business or

as a community?

When are you holding back from expressing your love for people around you?

Where might you be more loving towards other people?

What if you tell people that you love them?

What if you don't bring more love into your work?

- -

SELF-COACHING AND REFLECTION

What do I love to do?

What holds me back from demonstrating my love to other people?

How might I be more loving as a leader?

What do my people love about me?

What do I love about my people?

What if I bring more love to our work achievements ?

What if I don't let people know that I love them?

MANAGING

"Can you manage to do this?" infers that you are less than able and might need help.
Many promoted 'managers' feel less than able and hesitate to ask for help.

LEADING A GROUP CONVERSATION

Are we "just managing" or are we more capable than we are allowing ourselves to be?

What help might we benefit from asking for?

Who might we offer help to at this time?

INSPIRING A ONE-TO-ONE CONVERSATION

Where do you feel you are being over-managed?

What are you ready to manage more of?

Who inspires you with their management style?

How do you need to show up as a manager?

What are you currently hanging on to that might be managed by someone else?

What if you were challenged to manager more?

What if you didn't need to micromanage?

- -

SELF-COACHING AND REFLECTION

What aspects of my role need to be managed more carefully?

How might I release some of the aspects of management that frustrate me daily?

Where might I manage less and lead more?

What is the minimum level of management I need to take on?

When might I delegate more management to other people?

What if I didn't need to play the manager role?

What if I better manage all the competing aspects of my life and work at this time?

M

MEANING

When you create meaning in everything you do, the world opens up to you in a purposeful way. Look for the meaning in each moment.

LEADING A GROUP CONVERSATION

What everyday things might we acknowledge as making our work meaningful?

How might we be more purposeful in our approach?

How might we create more meaning for ourselves and for other people?

M

INSPIRING A ONE-TO-ONE CONVERSATION

What does it mean to you to be part of this team, this company
or this community?

How might you find more meaning in your work?

Where do you want to make a meaningful difference?

When do you create meaning for other people?

Who means most to you as a friend, colleague or partner?

What if you inspire someone to make a meaningful difference?

What if something is missing for you in your work and life?

- -

SELF-COACHING AND REFLECTION

Where did I find and create the most meaning in my work today?

Where am I finding my work to be meaningless?

What does the next level of success mean for me?

How do I convey meaning to other people?

How does my work or business make a meaningful difference?

What if I do one thing tomorrow to make a meaningful difference?

What if I get pulled away from doing meaningful work?

M

MEASURING

- -

"I am struck again and again by how important measurement is to improving the human."

— Bill Gates

- -

LEADING A GROUP CONVERSATION

What measurements will be most useful to us?

Where might we not need to measure so much?

How does our work improve the human condition?

INSPIRING A ONE-TO-ONE CONVERSATION

How will you measure your success with this task?

What measures of improvement mean most to you?

Where are we measuring something that's not useful?

When do we need to agree what to better measure?

Who is measuring this effectively?

What if you didn't need to measure this all the time?

What if you came up with some new ways to measure this?

- -

SELF-COACHING AND REFLECTION

How do I measure success?

What measures of improvement are most important to me?

Where might I be measuring the wrong things?

When do I need to measure results on this?

Who needs to know what I'm measuring them on?

What if our measures are not telling us what we want to hear?

What if we stopped measuring this?

M

MEETINGS

Create a day or even a week with no meetings.

"It's not about the presentation, it's about the conversation!"

— aha moment for one of my clients, 2016

LEADING A GROUP CONVERSATION

What's the most radical step we might take to change our approach to meetings?

How might we make all meetings useful?

Where might we replace formal meetings with more purposeful conversation?

INSPIRING A ONE-TO-ONE CONVERSATION

What is your objective for this meeting?

What structure do you need to run a good meeting here?

Who really needs to be at this meeting?

When might you speak up more at meetings?

Where could you be better at running your meetings?

What if you don't need a meeting about this?

What if you cancelled all your meetings?

SELF-COACHING AND REFLECTION

What if I don't need to call a meeting for this situation?

Who do I need to invite to this meeting and who doesn't need to be there?

How might I run a better meeting?

Where can I eliminate any unproductive meeting?

When might I speak up more or speak less in meetings?

What if I could do away with all formal meetings?

What if I changed the way I experience being in a meeting?

M

MINDFUL

Our minds are full rather than mindful. Press pause and bring your mind to attention. Go slow to go fast.

LEADING A GROUP CONVERSATION

What would slowing down look like for us?

What might we be missing if we're moving too fast?

What's the one thing calling for our full attention?

INSPIRING A ONE-TO-ONE CONVERSATION

What's distracting you from your core focus at this time?

Where do you need to take more time for yourself?

How might you relax more?

When are you feeling overwhelmed?

Who might you ask to take some things off your plate?

What if you approached this in a more relaxed way?

What if you don't take action to address how stressed this is making you?

- -

SELF-COACHING AND REFLECTION

When do I notice that my mind is so full I'm no longer effective?

Where might I pay more attention to how overwhelmed I am?

Who might I ask for help or to whom might I delegate more?

How might I be more mindful about what I need to be effective?

What is distracting me at this time?

What if I were to develop a daily practice of reflection, meditation or relaxation?

What if my mind stays as *full* as it is now?

M

NEEDS

Need-ful does not mean needy. To be clear on what you need and to ask for it is to fill up your life.

LEADING A GROUP CONVERSATION

What do we need to be successful?

Whose needs are we fulfilling with this?

What do our clients truly need from us?

INSPIRING A ONE-TO-ONE CONVERSATION

What do you need?

What do other people need from you on this project?

What do other people not need from you any more?

How fulfilled are you at work?

What's your most important need at this time?

What if you have an unfulfilled need?

What if you ask for more of what you need?

- -

SELF-COACHING AND REFLECTION

What need did I fulfill for myself or for other people today?

Where do I have a need that's currently unfulfilled?

When did I ignore or neglect for myself or for other people today?

How might I fulfill an important need for myself tomorrow?

What's my most important need at this time?

What if I am in danger of neglecting my own needs?

What if other people's needs are more important than my own?

NO

- -

One of the most loving things you might do is to respect when someone tells you no.

- -

LEADING A GROUP CONVERSATION

What do we need to say no to?

What might we anticipate our clients would say no to?

How might we acknowledge and respect the no in our conversations?

INSPIRING A ONE-TO-ONE CONVERSATION

Where do you need to say no to taking on more at this time?

When did you last say no to something?

Who do you have problems saying no to?

How might it serve you to say no to this?

What is stopping you from saying no?

What if you don't say no to this?

What if saying no is the best thing you could do here?

- -

SELF-COACHING AND REFLECTION

Who am I afraid to say no to?

Where would it have been better for me to have said no today?

How might it serve other people for me to understand it is ok to say no?

What is stopping me saying no to this?

When will it serve me better to say no?

What if I don't say no to this?

What if saying no is easier than I think it might be?

OBSTACLES

What's really getting in the way? There's only one real obstacle: you, yourself. Yes, you. You are your only obstacle.

LEADING A GROUP CONVERSATION

How might we be creating obstacles for ourselves?

What's really getting in our way?

What if we didn't let anything get in our way?

INSPIRING A ONE-TO-ONE CONVERSATION

What seems to be the obstacle for you on this project?

Where do you anticipate an obstacle will show up?

What holds you back from success?

What obstacle do you keep encountering on this?

What seems to be your biggest obstacle to success?

What if there is an answer to this obstacle you're facing?

What if you can do more to overcome this obstacle?

- -

SELF-COACHING AND REFLECTION

Where am I holding myself back from true success?

What obstacles did I encounter today and how did I respond to them?

What obstacle might I encounter tomorrow and how will I deal with it?

Where do I tend to see or look for obstacles when there are none?

What's the one obstacle that I keep coming up against?

What if I overcome whatever seems to be my biggest obstacle?

What if there were no obstacles to what I'll do next?

OPENNESS

An open mind needs an open heart. Open means letting something enter or pass through you, without letting it get stuck in you.

LEADING A GROUP CONVERSATION

Where do we need to be more open to other people's ideas?

What are we really open to creating together?

How might we be more open-hearted with each other?

INSPIRING A ONE-TO-ONE CONVERSATION

How open are you to trying something different?

Where might you be open to learning more?

When do you find yourself closing down?

What will it take for you to be more open-minded on this?

Who are you not being open with?

What if you opened up your team to a new way of doing things?

What if you don't open up to change?

- -

SELF-COACHING AND REFLECTION

How open am I to new possibilities or solutions?

Where am I not open to something new?

Where might I ask more open questions to see where they lead?

When might I more openly share plans, strategies or changes that impact people?

Who makes me shut down my own thinking or ideas?

What if I could be more open to change?

What if I am too open and need to be more focused?

OPPORTUNITIES

There's always another way: look for opportunities before obstacles and the obstacles will shrink and disappear.

LEADING A GROUP CONVERSATION

What alternative way might be open to us?

What are the greater opportunities for us as a team?

If our fairy godmother waves her magic wand and grants us three wishes —

what will we ask for?

INSPIRING A ONE-TO-ONE CONVERSATION

What opportunities do you see for success here?

Who else might see different opportunities here?

What's the biggest opportunity you are facing at this time?

What holds you back from exploring new opportunities for this?

Where are the opportunities for you on this project?

What if anything were possible for you to explore?

What if you take the next opportunity you're offered?

SELF-COACHING AND REFLECTION

What opportunity did I respond to willingly today?

Where might I have missed an opportunity today?

What holds me back from exploring new opportunities when they show up?

Who might see some opportunities in this situation, that I could be missing?

Where are the opportunities for me in this situation?

What if I create more opportunity for me on this task or project?

What if I respond to the biggest, scariest, most exciting opportunity facing me at this time?

OWNERSHIP

Ownership means no excuses. "Own" has the same letters as won. Owners win.

LEADING A GROUP CONVERSATION

Where might we take more ownership of what we are creating together?

What excuses do we allow to hold us back?

What will full ownership feel like?

How will we know we are winning?

INSPIRING A ONE-TO-ONE CONVERSATION

How might you take more ownership in this situation?

What would full ownership look like for you here?

Where would you like to take more ownership?

Who owns this result?

What do you own about this situation?

What if you've had a hand in creating this result?

What if you took ownership where you are currently reluctant to do so?

- -

SELF-COACHING AND REFLECTION

Where did I take full ownership today?

When and why did I fail to take full ownership of something today?

What does ownership really mean to me?

Where might I take more ownership of my own actions and responses?

What happens when I don't fully own my actions and responses?

What if I create opportunities for other people to take more ownership?

What if I fully own my failures or limitations?

PERFORMANCE

Performance = Potential minus Interference

— Myles Downey, Effective Coaching

LEADING A GROUP CONVERSATION

What's interfering with our performance?

How might we create more potential for success?

What does "high performance" ultimately mean for us?

INSPIRING A ONE-TO-ONE CONVERSATION

What feedback do you need on your current performance?

Where are you happiest performing?

What do you need to perform at your best?

How might you need to ease off and put yourself under less pressure?

Who do you admire for their current performance?

What if you aspire to a greater level of performance?

What if you are currently performing below par?

SELF-COACHING AND REFLECTION

How well did I perform in face of today's challenges?

What current pressures may be impacting my performance?

How happy am I with my current level of performance?

What feedback do I need to ask for, on how my current performance is affecting other people?

Where do I want to stretch myself to higher levels of performance?

What if I aim for a higher level of performance?

What if I don't truly want to perform?

PLANNING

- -

There is planning that seems like control and there is planning to be fully present in order to respond to what is happening right now.

- -

LEADING A GROUP CONVERSATION

How flexible are we in responding to situations that show up unexpectedly?

If we ignore the plan for a moment, what do we see is really happening?

Where might less control help us move forward?

INSPIRING A ONE-TO-ONE CONVERSATION

How might it serve you to have a plan here?

How might you need to change your anticipated plan to achieve a better result?

What is your plan?

Who do you need to engage in this plan?

What might be the limitations of your current plan?

What if your plan succeeds?

What if your plan fails?

- -

SELF-COACHING AND REFLECTION

When might I stay too attached to one plan at the exclusion of other possibilities?

How might I find benefit in some degree of planning and how would it serve me or others?

What are the downsides of my current plan?

What might lie beyond the reach of my current plan?

Who needs to be involved in creating a plan for success?

What if my plan works out well?

What if my plan fails, how will I respond?

POSSIBILITIES

You already know what's possible. How might you know the impossible?

LEADING A GROUP CONVERSATION

What possibilities might we explore together?

What if the impossible is possible for us?

Where are our potential breakthroughs?

INSPIRING A ONE-TO-ONE CONVERSATION

What seems impossible to you in this situation?

Where might you explore further possibilities?

What if anything is possible here?

What gets in the way of you exploring what's possible?

What's the craziest, wildest, most impossible thing you could do on this?

What if it's really not possible?

- -

SELF-COACHING AND REFLECTION

What do I believe to be possible for my team, my business or my community?

How might I explore what currently seems impossible?

What if anything is possible here?

What stops me from believing something new is possible?

What gets in my way of exploring the impossible?

What if the impossible becomes possible?

PULLING OUT POTENTIAL

Great leaders listen deeply and ask questions to pull out the potential that lies in each person.

LEADING A GROUP CONVERSATION

What new questions might we ask ourselves going forward?

Where are we ready to lead on our own?

Where might we tap into potential not yet unleashed?

INSPIRING A ONE-TO-ONE CONVERSATION

What do you see as your potential for success on this project?

Where are you not using your full potential?

If you were to really stretch yourself, what would you potentially do, create or achieve?

What potential do you look for in your team?

Where is the potential success in this for you?

What if you have potential you haven't yet tapped into?

What if someone has the potential to help you with this?

- -

SELF-COACHING AND REFLECTION

How am I working to my full potential?

What potential lies in my team, my business or my community that needs to be pulled out?

Where is the potential in this project?

What potential do I have that is currently under-utilized?

Who do I potentially seek to become as a leader?

What if I am over-reaching my potential?

What if I was truly working to my full potential what would I be doing and creating?

PUTTING IN ADVICE

If you keep putting in your current expertise and advice, there is no space for creative thinking or new ideas.

LEADING A GROUP CONVERSATION

Where do we need new ideas in order to move forward?

How might we think differently in order to get a different result?

What lies beyond our current expertise and knowledge?

INSPIRING A ONE-TO-ONE CONVERSATION

What do you think might work here?

How do you suggest we move this forward?

When do I impose my answers on you and how does that make you feel?

Who else might you ask for input and ideas?

What if you don't have all the right answers?

What if you look at this differently than the way you've looked in the past?

What if you don't yet know everything you need for this project?

- -

SELF-COACHING AND REFLECTION

Where and when did I impose my answers on people today?

How might I be more open to hearing other people's views and ideas?

What is the benefit in listening for other people's solutions?

What if I am not the best person or the expert in this situation?

How might things be different if I am not attached to being right?

What if am I afraid to give my answers?

What if people don't need answers from me?

QUESTIONS

Great questions stop you in your tracks, open you up to what you need to hear and call you to a higher game.

LEADING A GROUP CONVERSATION

What questions are we afraid to ask ourselves?

What if we called ourselves to our biggest, boldest, scariest next step?

What is our higher game?

INSPIRING A ONE-TO-ONE CONVERSATION

What question have you not yet asked yourself about this task or project?

Who is asking a question you can't answer?

What question are you and your team not yet asking about this?

What's the toughest question you've been asked recently?

What's the scariest question you or your team could ask in this situation?

What if you could answer that one question you've been asking over and over again?

What if you don't yet have an answer?

- -

SELF-COACHING AND REFLECTION

What's my favourite question to ask other people?

What question do I hate to be asked myself and why do I resist it?

What question has followed me all my life?

How might I ask better questions that make other people really think in different ways?

What's the toughest question I need to ask myself at this time?

What question am I currently avoiding?

What question do I not yet know the answer to?

REALITY

"I have one major rule: everybody is right. More specifically everybody, including me, has some important pieces of the truth, and all of those pieces need to be honoured, cherished, and included in a more gracious, spacious, and compassionate embrace."

— Ken Wilber

LEADING A GROUP CONVERSATION

What pieces of the puzzle are we missing and who holds them?

How much work will it take to reach our dream outcome?

What reality do we need to face in order to move forward?

INSPIRING A ONE-TO-ONE CONVERSATION

What do you really think about this situation?

What's really happening here from your perspective?

How might you look differently at this?

Where might you be seeing something that's not real?

When will you believe in the reality of this?

Who might see this differently from you?

What if this is not real?

What if you created a different reality around this?

- -

SELF-COACHING AND REFLECTION

What's my reality here?

What am I really thinking, feeling, sensing or experiencing about this situation?

Where might I turn my dream or idea into realistic action?

How might I look at this reality in a different way?

Who might see this in a different way?

What if this is not true?

What if I could create a different reality here?

REFLECTION

The only true reflection of your leadership is how people experience and respond to you.

LEADING A GROUP CONVERSATION

How might I better serve you as a leader?

What do you want me to know about myself that I don't seem to already know?

How do we want our colleagues and clients to experience us as a

team of leaders?

INSPIRING A ONE-TO-ONE CONVERSATION

On reflection, what might have worked better for you in this situation?

When do you create time and space to reflect on your learning?

When you reflect on your success with this, how do you feel?

What reflections can you share with me regarding my leadership?

How will your success reflect on your team and company?

What if you reflect on what you feel good about in your work?

What if, when you look in the mirror, you see a different reflection than the one you expect?

- -

SELF-COACHING AND REFLECTION

When do I create space for reflection in my day?

How might I better reflect on my impact as a leader?

What are people reflecting back to me about my leadership?

When I reflect deeply on what I might do better, what do I hear?

On reflection, what did I do well today? What might I do better tomorrow?

What if my leadership is reflected back to me in the words and actions of other people?

What if I reflect into the future to uncover what's there?

RELATIONSHIPS

"Getting to the next level of greatness depends on the quality of our culture, which depends on the quality of our relationships, which depends on the quality of our conversations. Everything happens through conversations."

— Judith Glaser, Conversational Intelligence

LEADING A GROUP CONVERSATION

How might we strengthen our relationships as a team, with our colleagues or with our customers?

What is the next level of greatness for us?

Where do we need new or different conversations?

INSPIRING A ONE-TO-ONE CONVERSATION

Where do you have the strongest relationships in your team?

Which relationship are you currently challenged by?

Where might you need to build stronger, more productive relationships?

What's troubling you about any relationships at this time?

How might you improve your relationship with someone?

What if you could create one new relationship at this time, who would it be with?

What if you have outgrown this relationship and need to move away from it?

- -

SELF-COACHING AND REFLECTION

Which relationship surprised me today?

Who do I want to build a stronger relationship with?

Who am I struggling to have an effective relationship at this time and what's getting in the way?

Where might I invest more effort to create a productive relationship?

How healthy are my relationships with my team members at this time?

What if this relationship is taking more effort from me than I am able to commit to?

What if I seek feedback from my closest relationships?

RESISTANCE

"The way lies in softness and patience, as the softest water cuts through the hardest rock."

— Jonathan Lockwood Huie

LEADING A GROUP CONVERSATION

What if we took a softer, slower, approach to this?

How could this be easier for us?

How will letting go of resistance move us forward?

INSPIRING A ONE-TO-ONE CONVERSATION

What are you resisting at this time?

Where are you encountering resistance in your team members or colleagues?

What is it that you and your people are resisting in this situation?

What's the strongest point of resistance on this and how might you look at that differently?

What will it take to break through your resistance to this?

What if you discover what's on the other side of resistance for you?

What if there's some learning in the resistance you are encountering?

- -

SELF-COACHING AND REFLECTION

What am I currently resisting and why?

Who seems to be resisting me at this time?

What might I resist in order to be more successful?

Where am I encountering resistance to my ideas?

Who, on my team, appears to be most resistant and what might that person have to teach me?

What if I am resisting something?

What if I can't break through my resistance at this point?

RESOURCES

"Our human resources are like natural resources:
they're buried deep. You have to go looking
for them; they're not just lying around on the
surface."

— Sir Ken Robinson

LEADING A GROUP CONVERSATION

What resources do we need?

What's underneath the surface that will lead us to success?

Where might being more resourceful help us?

INSPIRING A ONE-TO-ONE CONVERSATION

What resources do you need to get this job done?

How might you be more resourceful on this?

Where do you lack the resources to get the job done?

When could you be more creative with the resources available to you?

What inner resources do you rely on when things get tough?

What if you are not fully using your inner resources?

What if there are no more resources to enable you to get this done?

- -

SELF-COACHING AND REFLECTION

What inner resources might I rely on to get me through this challenge?

Where might I use my inner resources to better success?

How might I be more resourceful here?

When am I allowing lack of resources to hold me back?

How might I be more creative with the resources available to me?

SELF-AWARENESS

Everything stems from your level of self-awareness and how you keep exploring what you know of yourself, especially through the eyes of other people.

LEADING A GROUP CONVERSATION

Where are our blind spots as a team?

What do we need to be more aware of?

How do our colleagues or clients describe us?

INSPIRING A ONE-TO-ONE CONVERSATION

What are you aware might be holding you back from full success?

When do you need feedback from other people to help you?

What are you working on to improve your own behaviours and responses at this time?

Where and how might I help you with some feedback?

Where do you think you might have some blind spots that are holding you back?

What if there's something you need to check in your own self-awareness?

What if you feel disappointed in yourself?

- -

SELF-COACHING AND REFLECTION

What was I aware of in my behaviours and responses to other people today?

Where did I not pay attention to my own behaviours and impact on other people today?

What questions might I ask myself about how I showed up today?

Where might I get trapped in my own convictions?

What blind spots might be holding me back?

What if I invite feedback from other people to raise my own self-awareness?

What if I let myself down today?

SOLUTIONS

"I would love to live
Like a river flows,
Carried by the surprise
Of its own unfolding."

— John O'Donohue, Poem: Fluent, Conamara Blues

LEADING A GROUP CONVERSATION

What would surprise us about each other?

How might being more fluid and flexible serve us?

How would we like this to unfold?

INSPIRING A ONE-TO-ONE CONVERSATION

What do you see as a solution in this situation?

How focused are you on finding a solution?

Who might have important contributions to make towards your solution?

When might you have missed a possible solution?

Where are you looking or not looking for a solution?

What if you haven't tried every solution yet?

What if someone else has the solution to your current challenge?

- -

SELF-COACHING AND REFLECTION

What was the most creative solution I created today?

Where might I need to look for different solutions?

When did I impose my own solutions today without inviting input from other people?

How might I encourage more solutions from other people?

Where am I holding back, waiting for the perfect solution?

What if there's no perfect solution and what might I try as a next step?

What if the solution isn't obvious to me?

STRATEGY

"Strategy is about making choices, trade-offs; it's about deliberately choosing to be different."

— Michael Porter

LEADING A GROUP CONVERSATION

What different choices might we make together?

What risk are we ready to take?

How might a different strategy for success lead us forward?

INSPIRING A ONE-TO-ONE CONVERSATION

How do you define strategy versus tactics?

Where does strategy inspire you?

What is your strategy for success on this project?

Who needs to be involved in defining the strategic way forward?

How might you get pulled off the desired strategic direction?

What if you could contribute more fully to our strategic success?

What if you don't agree with this strategy?

- -

SELF-COACHING AND REFLECTION

What does strategy really mean to me?

Where do I feel I am most strategic?

When could I be more strategic in my thinking and actions?

What distracts me from working at a strategic level?

How inspired am I when working at a strategic level?

What if I am more comfortable in tactics rather than strategy?

What if I don't define a clearer strategy for this project?

S

SUCCESS

Success is more than results. It's the feeling of achievement. The excitement of realizing a dream. It's the satisfaction of a fulfilled desire. It's the meaning of creating something good in our lives.

LEADING A GROUP CONVERSATION

What do we most desire as a team?

What excites and inspires us to achieve more?

How does our work make a difference in the world?

INSPIRING A ONE-TO-ONE CONVERSATION

What does success look like for you on this task or project?

Which success are you most proud of?

Where are you struggling to achieve success?

When are you challenging my definition of success, or someone else's?

What's holding you back from success at this time?

What if you could take one small step to achieve success?

What if this doesn't turn out to be successful?

- -

SELF-COACHING AND REFLECTION

What felt successful to me today?

Where might I have taken a different path to success?

What does success really mean to me?

How do I measure my own success?

Where am I challenged by someone else's definition of success?

What if I'm super-successful with this?

What if I don't really want this to be successful?

TEAMWORK

Every great team is a combination of unique individuals coming together, honouring, respecting and valuing each contribution

---

LEADING A GROUP CONVERSATION

How might we better acknowledge each other's talent and contribution?

Where might we be bolder in sharing our individual ideas?

How might we best leverage the uniqueness of our team?

INSPIRING A ONE-TO-ONE CONVERSATION

What do you love about being on this team?

Where do you see the challenges or limitations in this team?

How do you define team success?

Where might you contribute even more to your team?

Who else needs to be on this team?

What if your team is already performing well?

What if there's something getting in the way of your team working well?

- -

SELF-COACHING AND REFLECTION

How well did I contribute to my team today?

Where might I have listened better to my colleagues today?

How do I know what my team really needs from me?

When am I a great or not-so-great team member?

Who on my team seems to be challenged at this time?

What if I focus on one thing?

What if I don't want to be on this team anymore?

TIME

There are 60 seconds in each minute, 60 minutes in each hour, 24 hours in each day — it's for you to choose how to use them. Always.

LEADING A GROUP CONVERSATION

How might we slow down and make more progress?

What different choices might we make about how we use our time?

When we experience time as expanded and limitless, what can we achieve?

What if we focus on space and ease rather than being time bound?

INSPIRING A ONE-TO-ONE CONVERSATION

How effectively are you using your time?

What time do you need to carve out to focus on this task or project?

Who might help you get this done more effectively?

Where are you getting distracted or pulled off track?

What's the one thing you can change to make better use of your time?

What if you give priority to one thing at this time?

What if you don't change how you are using your time?

- -

SELF-COACHING AND REFLECTION

How did I make the best use of my time today?

What choices did I make that pulled me off track?

How might I make better time and priority choices tomorrow?

What's the one thing that needs my focus at this time?

Where might I change a habit in order to more effectively use my time?

What if there's one thing that I can choose to do differently with my time?

What if I don't see time as my problem?

TRUST

Truth and trust share the same word origins. To build trust, practice truth. You can always trust yourself when you trust your truth.

LEADING A GROUP CONVERSATION

How might we build even more trust with each other, with our colleagues or with our clients?

Where do we need to place our trust in order to move forward?

How well are we living up to the trust other people have in us?

INSPIRING A ONE-TO-ONE CONVERSATION

Who do you trust and distrust most around here and why?

When do you feel someone broke your trust?

What truth do you need me to hear?

How easy is it for you to speak your truth around here?

Where do you sense or experience a lack of trust?

What if you were more trusting on this?

What if you've broken someone's trust?

- -

SELF-COACHING AND REFLECTION

Where did I work from a strong sense of trust today?

When and with whom do I need to create a greater sense of trust?

How might I share my truth with other people?

With whom do I need to build a stronger sense of trust?

Where am I currently sensing a lack of trust?

What if I didn't hold back from speaking my truth?

What if I could find a way to build stronger trust in my team and in my business?

UNDERSTANDING

To understand means to stand amongst or close to another's perceptions. Our job is not to understand other people: we can do no more than seek to understand how the world looks through their eyes.

LEADING A GROUP CONVERSATION

What do we need to understand more clearly as we move forward?

How does the world look through the eyes of our colleagues and our clients?

What are the many different perspectives we stand among?

INSPIRING A ONE-TO-ONE CONVERSATION

What do you need to understand to be successful with this?

Where do you not yet understand this?

Who do you have difficulty understanding?

When is it a challenge for you to get a full understanding of the situation?

What might be missing from your understanding of this situation?

What if you sought more understanding?

What if you need to share your understanding with someone on this project?

- -

SELF-COACHING AND REFLECTION

What did I miss or not understand fully today?

Where do I need to slow down and seek a deeper understanding?

Who do I have difficulty understanding when they speak?

Who might not have understood fully what I wanted to convey today?

When might I lack full understanding of this situation?

What if I need to better understand this project?

What if I can't understand this fully?

UNSAID

"Leadership fails when something is left unsaid."

— Borrowed and adapted from Myles Downey who said that coaching fails when something is left unsaid

---

LEADING A GROUP CONVERSATION

What's being left unsaid within our team?

Who amongst our colleagues or clients might have something important to say?

How might leaving nothing unsaid support us in reaching our goal?

INSPIRING A ONE-TO-ONE CONVERSATION

What have you left unsaid on this topic?

Where might you speak up more?

What's in your mind that you need to tell me?

Who do you think might be leaving something unsaid?

What question do you want me to ask you?

What if you are holding back from asking me a question about this?

What if you are avoiding hearing something you don't want to hear?

- -

SELF-COACHING AND REFLECTION

Where did I leave something unsaid today?

How well am I listening for what is not being said?

What might I do better to uncover what's not being said?

When do I make up a story about what's not being said?

What's the one thing that I have left unsaid for too long?

What if I am holding on to something instead of saying it?

What if I hear what I don't want to hear?

VALUE

"The ultimate value of life depends upon awareness and the power of contemplation rather than upon mere survival".

— Aristotle

LEADING A GROUP CONVERSATION

Where and for whom might we create or deliver greater value?

How will we create more opportunities to be of value?

Where is the hidden value that we might uncover for ourselves and for other people?

INSPIRING A ONE-TO-ONE CONVERSATION

What do you value most about your team, your work, and this organization?

Where might you contribute more value?

When are you not realizing your full value?

What do you value in your colleagues?

How valued are you feeling at this time?

What if you have not yet reached your full value ?

What if there is no more value in this for you?

- -

SELF-COACHING AND REFLECTION

What do I value most in other people?

Where do I best contribute my value?

When might I focus too readily on cost versus real value?

With whom do I struggle to speak openly about money?

How might I create more value on this project?

What if there is no real value in doing this?

What if we don't realize the full value of this opportunity?

V

VALUES

- -

Look to how you spend your days, what you enjoy, who you are with, and what you aspire to: there you will find the values you truly live.

- -

LEADING A GROUP CONVERSATION

What values do we truly live in our team?

Where might these values stretch us?

How might we test ourselves further against these values?

INSPIRING A ONE-TO-ONE CONVERSATION

Where is the value in spending time on this task/project for you?

What creates real value for you, for your team and for your business?

When are you at your best in life and at work?

How are you able to live out your values in your workplace?

What team or organizational values fit best with your own values?

What if you find it challenging to stay true to your values?

What if it's your values that are holding you back in this situation?

- -

SELF-COACHING AND REFLECTION

What brings me the most joy?

Where and with whom do I spend most of my time?

What do I aspire to?

How did I live my values today?

How does what I value guide my decisions and choices?

What if I could contribute even more value on this project?

What if it's my values that are trapping or stopping me in this situation?

VISION

Since the human eye can see as far as the stars, our vision can stretch beyond the obvious.

LEADING A GROUP CONVERSATION

What lies beyond our current vision of success?

How might we make our vision even more exciting and inspiring?

What success can we see light years ahead of where we are now?

INSPIRING A ONE-TO-ONE CONVERSATION

What's your vision of personal success?

What do you visualize we could create here?

How aligned are you with the overall vision?

Where might we envisage a different outcome on this project?

When do you get pulled away from your own vision of success?

What if our vision is wrong?

What if our vision is fully realized?

- -

SELF-COACHING AND REFLECTION

What are my three visions for my own success: short-term, medium-term and long-term?

Where might I need to visualize a different outcome?

When might I be pulled off track from my vision?

Who else needs to be aligned with my vision?

What if my vision changes?

What if my vision isn't realized?

V

VULNERABILITY

"In refusing our vulnerability we refuse the help needed at every turn of our existence and we immobilize the essential, tidal and conversational foundations of our identity."

— David Whyte, Consolations

V

LEADING A GROUP CONVERSATION

How might it serve us to show more vulnerability?

What help do we need to ask for?

How might we look at vulnerability as a strength?

INSPIRING A ONE-TO-ONE CONVERSATION

What does vulnerability mean to you?

Where do you feel we are most vulnerable on this project?

Who do you think is most vulnerable and exposed in this situation?

When might you find strength in vulnerability?

How might you show more vulnerability?

What if you don't hold yourself back from being vulnerable?

What if vulnerability brings you to a breakthrough?

- -

SELF-COACHING AND REFLECTION

When do I feel most exposed and vulnerable in front of other people?

How might I have the confidence to show my vulnerability?

What makes me vulnerable?

Who do I admire for their vulnerability?

What if vulnerability is a strength?

What if I try to hide my vulnerability and see what happens?

V

WANTS

"Tell me what you want, what you really, really want and I'll tell you what I want, what I really, really want."

— Spice Girls, Wannabe

LEADING A GROUP CONVERSATION

The ultimate business and life plan comes from this question:

"What do you want to do, be, see, feel, experience, achieve, give, receive in your life?"

It may be the only question(s) you need to ask.

(the IC International Team Question 1997–2007)

W

INSPIRING A ONE-TO-ONE CONVERSATION

What do you really want for you and for your team?

Where are you missing something you want in your life?

What more do you want to create?

Where do you want something more?

When do you want something the most?

What if you wanted something different from what you've got?

What if you didn't have to want for anything ever again?

- -

SELF-COACHING AND REFLECTION

What do I really want to create in my life and business?

How might I commit more fully to something?

Where do I want something more?

Why do I want this?

What happened today that I don't want to happen again?

What do I want to create tomorrow?

What if I already have everything I want?

What if I didn't have to want for anything?

W

WAY FORWARD

"Do not follow where the path may lead, go instead
where there is no path and leave a trail."

— Muriel Strode

LEADING A GROUP CONVERSATION

What's another way for us to move forward?

What path have we yet to explore?

What trail will we leave behind us: what will we be known for?

INSPIRING A ONE-TO-ONE CONVERSATION

How will you move forward with this task?

What's getting in the way of you moving forward?

Whose help do you need in order to move forward?

Where might you look for new or different ways forward?

When have you been successful in similar situations?

What if there's nothing holding you back from moving forward with this?

What if you don't need to move this forward?

- -

SELF-COACHING AND REFLECTION

What is my way forward on this challenge?

Where else could this go?

When might I look for new directions to move forward?

How did I move my business forward today?

What is the one next step my team needs to move forward with this project?

What if there's something getting in the way of moving forward?

What if this is not the only way forward?

W

WILL

"I will" surpasses could, or would, or should, or maybe, or probably, or might.

LEADING A GROUP CONVERSATION

What will we create together?

What gives us the will to take bigger steps?

What one big step will we take?

INSPIRING A ONE-TO-ONE CONVERSATION

What will it take for you to be successful with this task or project?

Where will you take your next step?

What action will you take to move this forward?

How much free will do you have on this?

When do you avoid taking action?

What if you don't achieve this goal?

What if there's nothing really holding you back?

- -

SELF-COACHING AND REFLECTION

What did I not have the will to tackle today?

How will I take action tomorrow?

Where am I lacking the willpower to make something happen?

What will it take for me to take the action that I've been avoiding?

How might I better exercise my free will in this situation?

What if I don't achieve this goal?

What if other people don't want to make this happen?

W

WISDOM

"The only true wisdom is knowing you know
nothing."

— Socrates

LEADING A GROUP CONVERSATION

What if we start from the point of knowing nothing?

If what we know is only a small part of what's possible, what else might be true?

When we are open to what we don't know, what might we discover?

INSPIRING A ONE-TO-ONE CONVERSATION

What confidence do you have in this approach?

Who do you know with more wisdom on this topic?

What does your inner wisdom guide you to do here?

When have you learned something in the past that you could use here?

How would you apply more wisdom to this situation?

What if your inner wisdom is wrong?

What if you don't trust your inner wisdom on this?

- -

SELF-COACHING AND REFLECTION

Who is the wisest person I might talk with about this?

Where might it be wise for me to pause before taking action?

What wisdom have I gathered from experience that I might apply here?

Why is this happening, why is this really happening?

How might I be being naïve or unaware here?

What if I listened more to my inner wisdom on this?

What if I'm not the wisest person around here?

W

X-RAY

"Have you ever listened to people from the inside? Listened so close you can hear their thoughts and all their memories. Hear them think from the places they don't even know they think from?"

— from the movie, *Powder*

LEADING A GROUP CONVERSATION

How might we listen more deeply to each other?

If we had the superpower of listening inside ourselves, what would we hear?

What crazy possibilities might be waiting to be heard?

X

INSPIRING A ONE-TO-ONE CONVERSATION

What's your inner voice telling you about this situation?

Where might you be missing something here?

When might you listen more deeply?

How might you not be seeing what's behind the surface?

Who do you need to be more aware of?

What if you are missing something you need other people to hear?

What if you could cut through the confusion in this situation and hear what might become clear?

- -

SELF-COACHING AND REFLECTION

What do I hear when I really listen to my inner voice?

Where am I not seeing beyond the surface in this situation?

How do I know what I don't know?

Whose clearer perspective do I need on this ?

When have I relied on my inner guidance?

What if I could see through the confusion in this situation, what might become clear?

What if I'm missing some details that x-ray vision could reveal to me?

X

YOU AND I

The space between you and me can connect us or push us apart. In-to-me-see (intimacy)

LEADING A GROUP CONVERSATION

What's really happening in the space between us?

How might we step more fully into the space where you and I come together?

What might we more consciously create together?

INSPIRING A ONE-TO-ONE CONVERSATION

What do you need from me to be successful?

When are you most concerned?

Where are you focusing your efforts at the moment?

What's on your mind?

How might I help you more?

What if you asked more often for what you need?

What if you can't make a strong connection with someone?

- -

SELF-COACHING AND REFLECTION

Where or with whom did I feel truly seen or heard today?

Who might I have not truly seen or heard as an individual today?

When might I focus more on each person as an individual?

How well do I see each person on my team for the individual contribution they make?

What might I do to better focus and inspire each person I meet?

What if I ask for more of what I need?

What if I keep using the generic we and it's not clear who I really mean?

Y

ZEN: IN YOUR ZONE

"Zen is not merely a system of thought. Zen infuses our whole being with the most pressing questions we have."

— Thich Nhat Hanh

LEADING A GROUP CONVERSATION

What questions infuse and absorb us in our work?

What most pressing question calls for our attention?

What might emerge when we work fully in our zone of inspiration?

Z

INSPIRING A ONE-TO-ONE CONVERSATION

What aspects of your work feel most "in your zone"?

Where do you best relax, renew and re-energize?

Who are you with when you are most relaxed, open and inspired?

When do you make the time to meditate, do yoga, enjoy nature, play sport, or relax with your family?

What if you could find a way to spend more time "in the zone"?

What if you were too busy to ever take real downtime?

- -

SELF-COACHING AND REFLECTION

When do I feel most inspired and in my zone?

With whom do I feel most relaxed and in my zone?

What do I need to do differently to be more "in my zone"?

Where is the best place for me to relax, renew and re-energize?

What if I spent more time in meditation, yoga, sport or in nature?

What if I never create the time to be fully inspired or in the zone?

Z

"When people engage in conversations,
commitments are made, and spaces of possibility
are opened up."

— Fernando Flores

I don't imagine you'll read this book from front to back without stopping. In fact I hope you don't. I trust you will pick it up and flip it open to find questions that really serve you daily, conversation by conversation. I trust you see new things happen because of those conversations. I trust you enjoy being a questioner rather than an answerer. And I trust you'll discover how to craft your own questions and create your own inspiring conversations, by adapting the style and formats of the questions in this book.

If you do, I know your questions will open up vital conversations.

Conversations that invite you into leadership. Conversations that invite you into new ways of being, where you speak up and ask the questions you haven't asked before. Questions which call you to action. Questions which invite you to become more of yourself. Questions which —- as David Whyte says in his poem Sometimes —- are patiently waiting for you and have no right to go away.

It is both our greatest challenge and our greatest opportunity to step into these questions — disruptive, uncomfortable and yet thrilling as they may be.

You will create new results for yourself, your team and your business when you start each day, each meeting and each conversation, with a new question from the pages of this book.

Hold it close by you. Keep it on your desk. Let it get dog-eared and coffee splattered with use. Carry it with you. Share it with colleagues. Let other people get their hands on it. Let this book itself be a conversation starter. Let it help you experience conversations you haven't stepped into before now.

Conversations to inspire you and everyone around you.

Aileen Gibb.

SOMETIMES

Sometimes
if you move carefully
through the forest,

breathing
like the ones
in the old stories,

who could cross
a shimmering bed of leaves
without a sound,

you come
to a place
whose only task

is to trouble you
with tiny
but frightening requests,

conceived out of nowhere
but in this place
beginning to lead everywhere.

Requests to stop what
you are doing right now,
and

to stop what you
are becoming
while you do it,

questions
that can make
or unmake
a life,

questions
that have patiently
waited for you,

questions
that have no right
to go away.

– David Whyte
from *Everything is Waiting for You*
©2003 Many Rivers Press
and *River Flow: New & Selected Poems*
©2006 Many Rivers Press

For this book I've called upon on almost two decades of conversations with my clients and I dipped into some of my favourite readings from authors who have inspired me to look at situations through new eyes. I sought to honour everyone from whom I borrowed a quote or idea and worked conscientiously to secure the appropriate permissions for various pieces. I was granted permissions from the following publications:

Csikszentmihalyi, Mihaly - *Flow* - 1991, Harper Perennial Edition, a Division of Harper Collins Publishers.

Chodron, Pema - *The Places That Scare You* - 2001, Shambhala Publications Ltd, Boulder, Colorado

Frankl, Victor - *Man's Search for Meaning* by Viktor E. Frankl Copyright © 1959, 1962, M1984, 1992 by Viktor E. Frankl Reprinted by permission of Beacon Press, Boston

Glaser, Judith - *Conversational Intelligence: How Great Leaders Build Trust and Get Extraordinary Results* - 2014, Bibliomotion Inc, MA.

O'Donohue, John - Fluent poem from *Conamara Blues* - 2000, Transworld Publishers, a division of Random House Group Ltd.

Secretan, Lance - *Reclaiming Higher Ground*, 1996 - MacMillan Canada.

Turkle, Sherry -Excerpt(s) from *Reclaiming Conversation: The Power of Talk in a Digital Age* by Sherry Turkle, copyright © 2015 by Sherry Turkle. Used by permission of Penguin Press, an imprint of Penguin Publishing Group, a division of Penguin Random House LLC. All rights reserved.

Whyte, David - *Sometimes* poem published in *Everything is Waiting for You - 2003*, Many Rivers Press, Langley, WA.

Whyte, David - *Consolations, The Solace, Nourishment and Underlying Meaning of Everyday Words* - 2015, Many Rivers Press, Langley, WA.

Whyte David - *Sweet Darkness* poem Published in *House of Belonging* - 1997, Many Rivers Press, Langley, WA.

Where I've used a quote, attributed to a name, but with no book referenced, you can assume I've taken it from one of the quote pages to be found on the internet. My assumption is that such quotes are in the public domain and don't require me to seek further permissions.

In this process I did discover that sometimes these quotes are not attributed to the correct source. For example I have used the often-quoted *"Do not follow where the path may lead, go instead where there is no path and leave a trail."*

Most common usages attribute these words to Ralph Waldo Emerson. One of my editors, however, identified it as attributable to Muriel Strode whose actual words were *"I will not follow where the path may lead, but I will go where there is no path and I will leave a trail."*

Should you, reader, be aware of, or come across any other such corrections to quotes which I have used, I'd appreciate you sharing that learning with me so that I may correct them in future editions.

There are also a couple of references to pieces I've heard on one of the many podcasts I listen to. Since I can't identify the exact source without re-listening to everything on my iphone, I firstly apologize for lack of attribution, and secondly, ask that if you recognize any of the sources, please let me know so that, again, I might give them full attribution in future editions.

Despite numerous attempts to obtain permission from Myles Downey for the references I've made to his work, no response was forthcoming so I've taken the liberty of using the pieces with full acknowledgement of their source (EFFECTIVE COACHING - 2002, Texere Publishing, London) and again ask that anyone authorized to grant formal permission for this piece gets in touch with me to correct this omission. Thank you.

The remaining provocative statements at the start of each section, which look like quotes but with no source attribution, are pieces I've heard myself say over the years. Some of them have become regular parts of my conversations with clients to provoke different perspectives and insights. One of my clients once called these "Aileen-isms."

Of course it is entirely likely that, even when I think these are my own words, they have been inspired by other reading, writing or listening from my own learning journey. I've tried my best to remember where and when I was inspired by sources relative to any of these pieces. I take full responsibility for any unintentional errors in anything I've said or written and will gladly ensure any corrections are made for future editions.

Thank you.

Asking Great Questions, invites you to listen and leads you into great conversations. Here are a few of my favourite books that invite further exploration and understanding of the importance of questions and conversation:

Berger, Warren - *A More Beautiful Question - The Power of Inquiry to Spark Breakthrough Ideas* - 2014, Bloomsbury, NY

Diggins, Gary - *Tuning the Eardrums - Listening as Mindful Practice* - 2016, Friesen Press, Canada

Gibb, Aileen - *Voices: A Coaching Story to Inspire your Future* - 2016, BC Allen Publishing, Portland, OR

Groysberg, Boris and Sling, Michael - *Talk Inc, How Trusted Leaders Use Conversation to Power their Organizations* - 2012, Harvard Business School Publishing

Wheatley, Margaret J. - *Turning to One Another - Simple Conversations to Restore Hope to the Future* - 2002 - Berret-Khoeler Publishers Inc, San Francisco

Zeldin, Theodore - *Conversation - How talk Can Change our Lives* - 1998 - The Harvill Press, London

Gratitude.

There are many, many people with whom I've shared an exploration of questions over the years. In particular I am grateful to the many clients — leaders both formal and informal — who've stepped into those questions with me. To Ian Wallace who taught me to shift my own perspectives and to question more deeply; to Gary Diggins who introduced me to the power of deeper listening and for sonic inspiration and friendship; to my uniquely phenomenal team at Inspirational Coaching International for the ten years of questioning and fabulously intense and insightful conversations; to my own coaches, past, present and future who support me to give voice to the questions inside me and that I need to ask myself; and to Karina, Cam, Jane, Mel, Scott and the team at Rocky Mountain Soap Company in my adopted home of Canmore, Alberta for trusting me with their leadership journey and for experimenting with the questions to build their own inspiring and mission-driven culture of conversation.

Thanks to Margo, Jodi, Gary and the team at Ben Allen publishing for reading the earlier editions of this book. And a big thank-you to Lieve Maas at BrightLightGraphics.com for creating such a beautiful cover and design — and for totally nailing it first time. You all helped me stick with it and overcome the challenges of working through the minute details that enabled this book to make its way into the world.

Thank you.

ABOUT THE AUTHOR

AILEEN GIBB

By her early forties, Aileen Gibb had risen through a corporate career including Human Resources, Sales and General Management in both private and public sector organizations, before moving into consulting and ultimately creating her own experiment in business with the entrepreneurial start-up of Inspirational Coaching International. At one point she remembers consulting with a leadership guru and being offended when he described her as a 'reluctant leader'. After some time she came to realize that she was indeed reluctant to follow the traditional path of a leader who exercised power over other people, controlling and telling them what to do. If that were to be leadership, then she wanted no part of it. Instead she followed her vision of inspired leadership which connected, respected, honoured and nourished the potential growth that each person could bring to an organization and she adopted a style of leadership based on her concept of 'pure' coaching which relies on the power of open questions, listening and heartfelt connection between colleagues. This experiment with her own company saw her build a coaching business with an amazing core team, a network of associates and client companies large and small around the globe. Everywhere she went, the power of conversation was evident. People wanted to be heard. Wanted to be free to express their ideas and to be part of something bigger than themselves. To ask questions and to listen deeply into what could be possible for them and their businesses. She and her business partners felt honoured to do work which was essentially human in nature and which got to the heart of who people really are. Aileen continues this work today as a Master Masteries Coach and works mainly one-to-one with leaders who are seeking to build the new-style, mission-driven, businesses of tomorrow and who appreciate that it all starts with the questions they ask themselves. From time to time, Aileen invites groups of these leaders to grow, learn and create together in a week-long intensive which takes place in renewing environments such as the Rocky Mountains of Alberta where she lives, or near the coastlines of her Scottish homeland. Aileen's first book, *VOICES* has been read by many as a coaching story to inspire the future. You can follow Aileen's work and opportunities to learn with her at www.aileengibb.com as well as on Facebook, Twitter and on LinkedIn. Email her with your questions aileengibb@icloud.com.

DOWNLOAD THE MOBILE APP NOW

This book is designed to sit on your desk as a visual reminder to ask a great question.

I realise though that you will likely not want to carry it around with you everywhere — and so I'm delighted to let you know it's also available as a handy APP so that you always have a great question at hand for any situation. And there's a space for you to capture all your favourite questions to use time and again.

Made in the USA
Monee, IL
18 February 2020